— Sotheby's – Garden
Day . N.Y.C
(10 July '95)

— Note:
GRENOUILLE · RESTAURANT
3 E 52ⁿᵈ St.
N.Y.C
(212) · 752 · 1495
Lunch : 12 - 2³⁰ pm
Dinner : 5⁴⁵ - 11¹⁵ pm –

THE FLOWERS OF LA GRENOUILLE

Dear Ana

THE FLOWERS OF
LA GRENOUILLE

I hope that this little
book will give you
many days filled
Charles Masson
with beauty and flowers
All my best

Charles

Clarkson Potter/Publishers
New York

A portion of the proceeds from this book will be donated to the Samuel Waxman Foundation for Cancer Research at Mount Sinai Hospital in New York City.

All photographs by Oberto Gili except:
Charles Masson: pages ii, 16, 54
Horst P. Horst: pages 6, 10, 26, 33, 50–51, 69, 80
Tom Eckerle: pages 70–71
Edward Addeo: page 80
All illustrations by Charles Masson except:
Bernard Lamotte: page 15

Published by Clarkson N. Potter, Inc., 201 East 50th Street, New York, New York 10022. Member of the Crown Publishing Group.

Random House, Inc. New York, Toronto, London, Sydney, Auckland

CLARKSON N. POTTER, POTTER, and colophon are trademarks of Clarkson N. Potter, Inc.

Manufactured in Singapore

Design by Howard Klein with Maggie Hinders

Library of Congress Cataloging-in-Publication Data

Masson, Charles.
    The flowers of La Grenouille / by Charles Masson;—1st ed.
    1. La Grenouille (Restaurant) 2. Flower arrangement. I. Title.
SB449.M3565/1994
745.92—dc20
93-32753

ISBN 0-517-59057-3

10 9 8 7 6 5 4 3 2 1

First Edition

CONTENTS

"Bois de la vie."

"Drink life."

TO PAPA

This book is dedicated to my father.

The bounty of food my father shared with us in the restaurant and throughout his life was not only food for the stomach and the palate but food for the spirit as well. In addition, his great love of flowers taught us how life could be lived more beautifully. He opened the senses of those around him, to whom he would say, *"Bois de la vie"* ("Drink life").

My father was a very strong man all of his life and then suddenly he became ill and died. I was nineteen. I knew little about the restaurant that my father and mother had built, and even less about flowers. But I knew this much: I could help my mother and family more in the restaurant than I could in any other business. I left college and began working at La Grenouille.

Having been raised in a family where the restaurant was the center of our lives, it became increasingly clear how I would eventually become a restaurateur. At times I would remember things my father had talked about: details, always those little incessant details that make a restaurant tick. I felt unsure, but I felt my

father's presence all of the time—as I still do. Even now, I am never alone. His remarks, his thoughts, his spirit, become clearer to me in the details of the dining room, the kitchen, the flowers, everything.

I remember the first few times I tried arranging the bouquets at La Grenouille. Given my ignorance about flowers, it wasn't easy. My Aunt Monique, who had worked with my father, helped me a lot in the beginning. But it was consistently frustrating for me because I kept wondering why the flowers didn't last. I was obviously doing something wrong.

It was essential to remember the things my father did with his flowers, I realized, or I would have to learn the hard way. So my education on flowers, as in the restaurant in general, has been a combination of remembering what my father said and learning through trial and error—many errors.

As the years went by, I learned more and more about the restaurant and the flowers that my father loved so much. Then one night in the room upstairs, I saw leaves and petals covering the

floor. The trail led to under my desk where my dog, Pancho, was hiding. His belly pumped in and out as he breathed heavily.

"Come out of there, Pancho!" As he heard me, he wedged himself as far as he could underneath that old wooden desk. I pulled him out by his hind legs and turned him over. He crossed his paws over his muzzle to hide parts of a fat, swollen face. His eyes were puffed up like the fish you see in the aquariums of a pet store.

He was still chewing on something.

I opened his mouth and removed what was left of a flower. Then I looked around and found near the table beside the desk a spilled vase, a puddle of water, and several headless stems strewn across it. No flowers.

I rushed Pancho to the animal medical hospital, where after a few shots he was back to normal. The vet looked at me in a strange way and said, "Does your dog always eat flowers?" But the way he asked it sounded more like "Why do you feed your dog flowers?"

"I guess he likes flowers," was my answer.

I thought about that and I realized that our love for flowers runs deep throughout the whole family. But I never imagined I would come to like flowers so much that one day I would write about them.

THE DAY PANCHO ATE THE FLOWERS.

CHAPTER I

A FEAST
OF
FLOWERS

It all began with my mother. Back in 1962, my father had been away much of the time working on a ship, the S.S. *Independence*. My father liked sailing and I guess he enjoyed the independence, literally.

My mother knew my father better than anyone. And she knew how to bring him back to shore. She felt it was time to bring out what was inside of him after all those years.

My mother walked all over New York City looking for a restaurant. Finally she stumbled on a wreck being auctioned in Midtown and cabled my father while he was on the *Independence* on a calm sea. The message read: "Congratulations, you are the owner of 3 East 52 Street."

My father returned to New York, and when he saw the building at 3 East 52nd, he was stunned. He couldn't believe my mother had signed the papers for it. Just the idea of opening a restauant, let alone in such a place, was insane.

"Just turn on the lights."

My father's life had been spent working in restaurants everywhere, beginning at childhood in his mother's restaurant, Le Grand Select, in Belfort, France.

From his mother, a great cook and a very hard worker, my father began to learn the restaurant business. When he was thirteen, he left home for good, and in order to survive, he relied on what he knew. He worked in various kitchens and dining rooms wherever he traveled. Then, in 1938, the World's Fair opened in New York. The great Henri Soulé represented French gastronomy in the Pavillon Français. My father worked for him there, and that's when my father discovered America.

My father became an American citizen and when the war broke out, he served in the United States Army in Hawaii. He learned a great deal from the army's no-nonsense organization. On the fertile volcanic soil outside his kitchen he planted a prolific garden. There were all sorts of fruits and vegetables: tomatoes, bananas, beans, pineapples, herbs, and more. He also grew flowers. Papa spent two of the best years of his life in Hawaii, and then returned to New York and became maître d'hôtel for Henri Soulé at Le Pavillon in Manhattan.

Meanwhile, my mother, who is not to be deterred in anything she has set her sights on, had decided to come to America after World War II. After securing a visa, she booked her passage on the *New Amsterdam* and arrived in New York in 1949 with a borrowed thirty dollars in her pocket.

It was in New York that my parents found each other and married. For three years they operated a small restaurant in the Berkshires and during winter months they went to Florida, working at various restaurants toward what amounted to a collective nervous breakdown.

Taking a break from the restaurant business, my father went back to sea aboard the *Independence* while my mother remained in New York, working at Christian Dior until 1962, when she sent that fateful telegram.

Back in New York, my father saw all of the work that had to be done just to open the restaurant, and then naturally all of the work that had to be done to *keep* it open. Even with all of his experience

My mother, Gisèle, and Spotty on the thirtieth anniversary of the restaurant.

behind him, my father saw ahead of him the biggest and most difficult challenge of his life.

The second part of that unforgettable telegram had been: "Need name to put in lease." His reply was: "Call it La Grenouille." *"Ma petite grenouille"* ("my little frog") was a nickname my father had given my mother long ago. All of the things he loved most in life would pour out of his heart into this little house at 3 East 52nd Street; so naturally he would call it La Grenouille.

The restaurant opened its doors on December 19, 1962, on a quiet night in the midst of a snowstorm. From the first day there were flowers, just a few roses here and there, but few as they were, this was to be the birth of a tradition.

La Grenouille grew by the day with warmth and beauty. It was not to be a restaurant where only food would be served. For my father there was food for the palate and there was more. There was the service he learned through his travels working in many fine restaurants. There was the art of the table. But as important to him was the life around the table: the art of living. This life he was about to share with all those who dined at La Grenouille.

One afternoon after lunch had been served, when all of the guests were gone, my mother and father sat down in the empty dining room to have their own lunch. They sat on the red banquette directly across from the window. A ray of sunlight pierced through the window and its filmy curtains, shining in their faces.

My father realized this must be uncomfortable for his guests. It was a problem to be solved. He thought of a few possible solutions. Heavier curtains would block out too much of the daylight, making the room look dark on a sunny day. Tint the windows? Out of the question. Suddenly it clicked. Flowers! A massive bouquet of flowers right there would do it!

He rushed out and bought a tall carved crystal vase at Baccarat. When he returned, he created a huge bouquet of flowers that would do far more than just block a stubborn ray of sunlight in the days to come.

My father's eyes must have traveled around the dining room from a new perspective. Before long, one bouquet led to another, and they were no longer there just to block the sun. The bouquets grew. While some people thought it was silly, others appreciated it very much. Salvador Dalí, sitting in a corner with his head in a bouquet, told my father, "Monsieur Masson, you throw money out the windows, but it comes back to you through the doors."

My father's sudden death in 1975 changed my life. I left college and started my own journey as a restaurateur. Papa had lived the restaurant. He breathed it. I quickly began learning about that life. On the eve of his death Papa spoke to me about many things—his life, our family—and then he talked about the restaurant. He said simply, "You can't run a restaurant without being there. Someone of the family must be there—even if all you do is turn on the lights in the morning. Just be there and you'll see. "

"Just turn on the lights." That short, simple message has never left me. The next morning and many mornings that followed, I did just that. I turned on the lights and I tried to learn as much as I could. The restaurant lived on, thanks to my mother, my family, friends, and the help of some very faithful employees. There I was at six-thirty in the morning learning what Papa meant by "turning on the lights."

Ismael, Rafael, and Colon were dishwashers who loved my father. They had worked devotedly for him almost since the day the restaurant opened. In their own way, they showed me what my father took care of every morning. I learned that the ovens were cleaned first, then the floors, walls, shelves—everything in the kitchen scrubbed to a shine. Then came the sidewalk, the windows, and the canopy. The dining room mirrors were polished, the chandeliers cleaned, the carpets and settees vacuumed, service carts waxed.

Every inch of the restaurant was cleaned daily. The silverware was also polished each day and burnished once a week; the stemware and china were checked for chips and scratches. The cooks started reducing their stocks in the early hours of the day also. As I watched Colon checking the light bulbs in the ceiling I learned that there are more than two hundred bulbs throughout the dining area. The importance granted to every minute detail was the essence of a smoothly run course that began once the doors opened to the first customers at noon. Through these

morning rituals I was learning that a restaurant is as perishable as the food it serves, and must be recreated each and every day.

And, of course, there are the flowers. Fresh flowers arrive daily to add to this early-morning renewal.

Thirty or so glasses are cleaned every morning and filled with fresh water. Small bouquets will be made in them. Each one of them will be placed on a table covered with a well-pressed white

linen tablecloth. The waiters will set sparkling china and silverware on each table. And of course there are the large bouquets to make in the dining room. When the restaurant opens its doors every day for its first customers, everything looks fresh yet simple. My father loved simplicity and spontaneity.

Just before closing the restaurant on some Saturday nights, after a long day of hard work, my father would bunch up most of the flowers and roll them up in tablecloths. He brought the tablecloths full of flowers home. I can only imagine my mother's expression when in the wee hours of the morning my father would spill an immense carpet of flowers onto the living room floor.

As a child I remember waking up on Sunday mornings to see and smell the beautiful bouquets he created in the house. Sunday was a day of rest; the restaurant was closed. But even at home my father still had flowers everywhere. And then he would open the refrigerator and cook up a feast out of the simplest ingredients. It was all very spontaneous, nothing calculated or pretentious. It just happened, and it happened beautifully.

That's the way Papa was. He was not only a great man and a great artist, he was above all a great father.

"Avant de mettre les rideaux, il faut faire la cave."

❧

"Before you hang the curtains, you must first build the cellar."

Chapter 2

Composition
and
Color

"C'est du théâtre" ("It's theater"), he would say. He was right: dining is an experience not limited to the palate alone. "He" was Bernard Lamotte. He sat at a small table in the restaurant, sketching on a tiny pad while lunching and watching.

Bernard Lamotte was a very good friend of my father. He taught me, as he had taught Papa, much about painting. The lessons I learned about composition and color are priceless. Consequently, much of what I learned about composing a bouquet, I owe to Bernard as well.

Had my mother not signed those papers committing her and my father's lives to 3 East 52nd Street, I might never have met Bernard. As it turned out, it seemed inevitable that our paths should meet. Well before La Grenouille was born, in the very same location stood a large studio on the second floor where Bernard lived and painted. Bernard arrived in the United States at about the same time as my father, yet they didn't really know each other until later, when La Grenouille opened.

Before coming to America, Bernard had lived in the 15th Arrondissement in Paris, where my mother and grandmother lived. Later, he occupied that second-floor New York studio and painted the murals at Le Pavillon, where my father was working at the time.

When I remember Bernard and the times my father and I shared with him, I know that it was not coincidence, but rather fate that would make his life cross ours.

Once La Grenouille opened, Bernard would occasionally return to his old address to have lunch. It took some years before my father convinced him to return to his old home upstairs. With its high ceilings, skylight, fireplace, tall leaded windows, and white brick walls, it had many stories to tell. Bernard had been reluctant to awaken the past in those walls, those unforgettable evenings he spent upstairs around the fireplace with such friends as Jean Gabin, Antoine de Saint-Exupéry, Charles Chaplin, and Greta Garbo. He would talk fondly of those evenings, such as the time he hastily created a table out of two-by-fours for a large impromptu party for all of his friends. He even drilled holes in the top to place glasses and ashtrays. Everyone present signed their name on that table.

Finally, one day he went up the steps with my father. The past came alive when he opened the door of the apartment, and he opened an important chapter in the lives of my father and me. Papa and I learned a great deal upstairs in that studio. In that room we learned about composition and color.

In composition, Lamotte would use the same techniques as the Great Masters, drawing light, imperceptible lines over a painting to divide the canvas in halves, quarters, eighths, and six-

teenths to show the weaknesses of the painting. "Too busy in this area ... nothing there. ..." Sometimes he would take a painting, turn it upside down or reflect it in a mirror, and suddenly you would see quite clearly what was wrong with the balance, the composition.

Bernard also had a few important rules outlining what *not* to do. While they may seem to apply solely to painting, I feel these rules apply to other arts as well. The great restaurateur Fernand Point, once wrote, "The simplest dishes are the best," and, "Garnishes should be matched to a dish like a tie to a suit." These statements bring to light the absurdity of so many unharmonious dishes, fantasies protected under fashionable labels, dishes that fade away as quickly as they appear. Great dishes, classics, do not disappear; their harmony, their composition, puts them beyond fashionable trends.

Some of the rules Bernard taught me were simple: Avoid *égalité de valeur*— evenness of value. Bernard would point to a painting where there was no harmony, where colors fought one another. One or a few colors should dominate, he said, while the other colors, through their weaker tones and complementarity, should bring forth form and color, thus giving depth to the painting.

I have seen examples of the opposite, in which all of the colors clash; they are out of context with each other. I have noticed that this happens frequently in paintings of floral arrangements, where the flowers are in bold, vivid colors fighting for attention. There is no unity, no harmony, because there are too many ingredients, with little in common between them. I am always impressed by the fact that Rembrandt, Goya, and El Greco, among other Great Masters, used essentially three or four colors in their palettes from which they derived their full color spectrum. Their work is harmonious and real because they did *not* use every obtainable color at once. Their paintings have no *égalité de valeur*.

In his book *The Education of a Gardener*, Russell Page, the great gardener, wrote: "I enjoy designing austere gardens, using a very limited and simple range of materials and trying to create a harmony by carefully adjusted proportions."

Avoid *égalité de volume*—evenness of volume. Bernard taught me not to make shapes compete with one another. If you want an object (or a mass of objects) to take center stage, you do *not* put this object next to another object of the same size. One mass of objects or one object should be helped by smaller accessories in order to dominate the picture. This creates depth, a true sense of space.

Avoid *symétrie*—symmetry. Avoid it! It kills any sense of movement. Whenever Bernard saw a painting with something too perfectly centralized, he would mimic someone holding a gun and shooting a bull's-eye. A painting divided by a central line, a

landscape where sky and land are of the same dimension, is boring and gives no depth. The land and the sky both collide in the middle. Half and half—end of story.

That is why choosing a vase is important. It is not only the flowers that you are looking at, but the object containing them as well. A bouquet of flowers is an entity; its container plays a decisive role. It will often dictate the physical confines of space and balance. It will tell you what is possible and what is not. It will tell you how many flowers can go into the vase without squeezing the stems and suffocating the flowers. It will let you know how far the branches, stems, and flowers can reach out of the vase without tipping the vase over.

When making a bouquet, I remember what Bernard told me about composition, about avoiding *égalité de valeur, égalité de volume,* and *symétrie.* If I overlook these basic rules and what I arrange does not look right, I start all over. It's easier to start anew than to fix a big mess. If you try to repair a big mistake, it will probably get worse and in the process you will waste a lot of time and flowers. The resulting bouquet may look tired and contrived instead of fresh and effortless.

What Bernard taught me regarding composition is to emphasize the main point of interest while using the less visible accessories to help it. Anything else might be superfluous, unnecessary, and if it is not necessary, don't use it.

Above all, Bernard always felt a painting had to tell a story. *"Il faut que ça me raconte une histoire."* In other words, it should come from the heart.

On color, Bernard taught us to keep the palette simple. To prove his point on accentuating or subduing color, he would pick up a piece of cardboard or paper, and with a few brush strokes demonstrate the effectiveness of the classic rule of *clair-obscur*, or using the contrast between light and dark tones to accentuate the subject. It is important to sense how colors work together. One fundamental rule on the interaction of colors is the color triangle. Using this triangle proves to be extremely helpful, especially for accentuating with contrasting or complementary colors.

The triangle is formed by three colors, red, blue, and yellow.

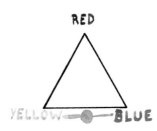

Red: The complement of red is green. The two other points of the triangle are yellow and blue. Mixed together, they make green, which is the complement of red. There are as many complementary shades of green as there are shades of red.

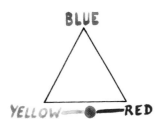

Blue: The complement of blue is orange. The two other points of the triangle are yellow and red. Mixed together, they make orange, blue's complement. There are as many shades of orange to complement as there are shades of blue.

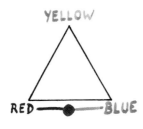

Yellow: The complement of yellow is purple. The two other points of the triangle are blue and red. Mixed together, they make purple, the complement of yellow. There are as many complementary shades of purple as there are shades of yellow.

When my father was asked to describe in a few words how he made a bouquet of flowers, he would say: "First, I start with color, then I make a pattern. Flowers in related colors make a happy family. Take red. What is mauve? A red and blue. What is orange? A red and yellow. Remember that light flowers say hello, dark flowers recede. Or use contrast to make your bouquet jump. If you don't have a variety of color, concentrate on shape. If you have only rosebuds, plunge a few stems in boiling water to rush them open. A bouquet may last four days or a week, but it will mature and change. The real eloquence comes as it opens."

Structure in a bouquet is very important as well; it becomes an integral part of the composition of a bouquet. If you look closely at a bird's nest you will notice how the twigs and stems hold each other in place perfectly—no wire, tape, glue, or nails. A bird's nest is a structural marvel.

I almost never use wire, or tape, or Oasis foam in my bouquets, unless it is absolutely necessary, such as in a very shallow container. Most flowers do better in just clean water, particularly those with tubular stems—anemones, daffodils, narcissus—and I like it best when the result doesn't look too arranged. A bouquet whose stems are secured ends up looking like a stiff, wired-up arrangement. If the first stems placed in the arrangement hold each other well, it becomes easy to control the position and movement of each flower as the composition progresses. And when wire or Oasis is not used, there will be more room in the late stages of the bouquet to add flowers, if necessary.

Although chicken wire is convenient because it quickly holds the flowers steady without the need to build or "knit" a structure of stems, I find that as I fill the bouquet with more flowers, I may no longer be able to see or feel the wire and therefore may inadvertently damage some stems by pushing them through the wiring instead of the spaces. In addition, Oasis or similar foams are not only unattractive (chicken wire seen through a crystal vase doesn't look great either!) but are also bad for some flowers, especially tubular-

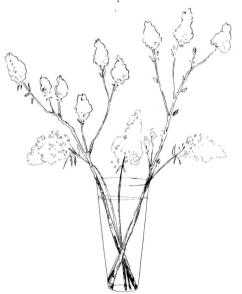

STRUCTURE CAN BE ACHIEVED BY CRISS CROSSING OR "KNITTING" STEMS TOGETHER.

stemmed ones. If you are arranging flowers for a party and are not concerned about their longevity, however, these aids can be convenient to use.

Structure can be achieved by crisscrossing or "knitting" the stems together. Knitting means continuously crisscrossing the stems throughout the bouquet so that each stem contributes not only to the structure of the bouquet but to its aesthetics as well.

It is possible to make huge arrangements without fastening or tying the vase down. Heavier branches work best in the heavier vases, usually those that can hold more water. I always use balance and the knitting technique, which locks

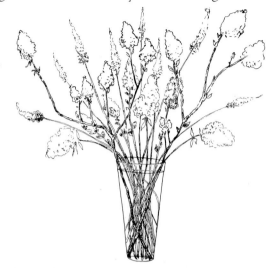

START WITH THE BIGGER BRANCHES AND FINISH WITH THE SMALLER ONES.

the stems tightly so that they cannot slip or move. I also move around the bouquet and work from all angles. This not only ensures proper weight distribution, but it makes me arrange the flowers from every viewing point. A sculpture should be seen from every angle. It is not two-dimensional. Neither is a bouquet. I start with the bigger stems and finish with the thinner, smaller ones. The structure from beginning to end is part of the form you give to the bouquet.

I remember Bernard saying: *"Avant de mettre les rideaux, il faut faire la cave"* ("Before you hang the curtains, you must first build the cellar"). That sentence sums up the importance of composition.

CHECK THE BOUQUET FROM EVERY
ANGLE STILL CRISSCROSSING THE STEMS AS STEMS
CONTRIBUTE TO THE STRUCTURE OF THE BOUQUET.

Think explosion—not implosion—when making a bouquet. A full bouquet should look voluptuous, never stuffed. When looking at the mass of an object, of a flower, I respect the space around it just as much as I do the space it occupies. Without that space the volume is meaningless. A few empty spaces are also necessary. They are like silent moments in a symphony.

A bouquet does not need to be immense to be effective. Respecting space, volume, proportions, and color will give grandeur to even the smallest bouquet. When I put flowers together, even just a few, the colors speak to me, just as the shape does.

From Fernand Point or Russell Page, Bernard Lamotte or my father, the language of composition is the same. It is the universal language of all the arts. And the most important message in that language is simplicity. It takes a lot of observation and practice to make anything look simple and natural.

Many artists have inspired me. Their works have taught me lessons in form, composition, and color. Through their work I have learned more about painting and sculpture. To me, flowers are a natural combination of both these arts. And flowers are the living food of the spirit; they are the symbol of life itself. That is why flowers are so important to me.

Flowers by Color

Whites agapanthus, almond blossom, amaryllis, anemone, anthurium, apple blossom, aster, astilbe, azalea, bouvardia, camellia, campanula, candytuft, Canterbury bell, carnation, chincherichee, chrysanthemum, clematis, columbine, cornflower (bachelor's button), cosmos, dahlia, daisy, delphinium, didiscus, dogwood, euphorbia, feverfew, freesia, gardenia, gerbera, genista, gladiolus, godetia, grape hyacinth (muscari), gypsophila (baby's breath), heather, hydrangea, iris, jasmine, larkspur, lilac, lily of the valley, lilies (Calla, Casablanca, Easter, Madonna, Mont Blanc), lisianthus, magnolia, narcissus (paper white), nerine, nigella (Love-in-a-Mist), nymphaea, ornithagalum, pansy, peach blossom, pear blossom, phlox, Queen Anne's lace, ranunculus, rhododendron, roses, scabiosa, snapdragon, stock, sweet pea, sweet William, statice (*latifolia*), stephanotis, tuberose, tulip, viburnum (snowball), wisteria.

Yellows and Oranges buttercup, calendula, California poppy, Chinese or Japanese lantern, chrysanthemum, cockscomb (celosia), columbine, dahlia, yellow delphinium, eremurus, eschscholtzia, euphorbia, freesia, gerbera, gladiolus, goldenrod, hyacinth, iris, japonica, lantana, lilies, lupine, marigold, nasturtium (capucine), pansy, phlox, ranunculus, roses, safflower, sandersonia, snapdragon, stock, sunflower, tulip, yarrow, zinnia.

Dark Orange to Brown anthurium, cattail (punk), chrysanthemum, cockscomb (celosia), coreopsis, dianthus, eremurus, freesia, gerbera, hydrangea (in fall), iris, lilies (Moulin Rouge), marigold, pansy, roses, zinnia.

Orange to Red
anthurium, carnation, chrysanthemum, cosmos, dahlia, fritillaria, gerbera, gladiolus, lily, nasturtium, peony, poppies, pyracantha (fire thorn), ranunculus, salvia, snapdragon, zinnia.

Reds
amaryllis, anemone, anthurium, carnation, cockscomb (celosia), dahlia, euphorbia, freesia, gerbera, gladiolus, godetia, hollyhock, ixia, lavatera, lilies, lobelia (*cardinalis*), peony, roses, snapdragon, stock, sweet pea, sweet William, zinnia.

Pinks
amaryllis, anemone, anthurium, aster, astilbe, campanula, Canterbury bell, carnation, chrysanthemum, bleeding heart (dicentra), columbine, cornflower, cosmos, dahlia, foxglove, freesia, gerbera, gladiolus, godetia, gypsophila (baby's breath), heather, hollyhock, hyacinth, hydrangea, larkspur, lavatera, lilies, lupine, peony, phlox, poppy, ranunculus, roses, scabiosa, snapdragon, stock, sweet pea, sweet William, tulip, verbena, zinnia.

Blues and Purplish Blues
agapanthus, ageratum (Blue Angel), allium, anemone, aster, bellflower, bergamot, brodaea, campanula, Canterbury bell, clematis, columbine, cornflower, cosmos, delphinium, didiscus, forget-me-not, gentian, gladiolus, grape hyacinth (muscari), hyacinth, hydrangea, iris, larkspur, nigella (love-in-a-mist), nymphaea, pansy, phlox, primula, scabiosa, sweet pea, thistle, veronica.

Purples
anemone, aster, campanula, Canterbury bell, columbine, cosmos, dahlia, delphinium, dianthus, freesia, gladiolus, heather, iris, larkspur, lavender, lilac, lupine, monkshood, pansy, roses, scabiosa, sweet pea, violet.

Greens

Bear grass, berries (almost any when not ripe), boxwood, eucalyptus, evergreens, ferns, holly, hydrangea (early stage), ivy, johnson grass, lemon leaves, mosses, palms, pine, privet, snow-on-the-mountain, Solomon's seal (small white flowers), viburnum, vinca vine, woodwardia.

These greens vary in shade and some are variegated. I occasionally use vegetables, shrubs, or herbs: artichoke (when flowering, it has a beautiful blue bloom at its top), corn with its stalk, hake, rosemary, sorrel.

A forest of greens and so many shades! That is because green is the dominant color in the natural world of plants. One could make a bouquet with different shades and textures of green alone.

"But did you speak to the flowers?"

CHAPTER 3

CONDITIONING

On occasional weekends my father would escape alone to
Florida. He would golf, fish, garden, walk on the beach, and be
very happy while becoming an instantaneous beach bum, barely
recognizable. On one such occasion during his absence from the
restaurant, the air conditioning in the dining room broke down
and the room was very warm.

My mother saw that one flower arrangement had suffered badly,
and courageously decided to resuscitate it. She bought some
tulips and tried to liven up the tired bouquet. Remembering my
father's tips on making a bouquet—on how to crisscross or
"knit" the stems—my mother went forward, cutting and knitting as best she could.

Now the bouquet looked much better—for a while. An hour
had not passed before she saw the salvaged bouquet wilt again.
Its tulips were drooping like old banana peels. Quickly she
called my father in Florida. She was lucky to reach him as he
did not spend much time near telephones while on his holiday.
My mother explained the dilemma and my father quizzed her:

"But did you cut and clean the stems?"

"Yes, of course I did!"

"But did you knit the stems?"

"But of course!"

"Was there enough water, was it clean?"

"Yes, yes."

The conversation went on until my father asked the portentous question:

"But did you speak to the flowers?"

No answer.

"... *Ma pauvre Gisèle*" ("... My poor Gisèle"). That was all my father had to say. That is, after all, what this business of a green thumb is about.

But the flowers had wilted not just because they had not been "spoken to." My mother had arranged the flowers without *conditioning* them.

Aside from talking to flowers, there are a few practical steps that have proven useful for making them last longer. Cut flowers need water, but they also need to be conditioned, and to be fed. Each kind of flower needs to be cleaned and recut in a certain manner. For instance, roses should be cut on a slant. Anemones should be cut straight across. For conditioning, roses need hot water; anemones, ice water. Then there are the ingredients mixed in this water which will strengthen and revitalize the flower after it is cut. Proper maintenance and conditioning are as important as arranging flowers beautifully. And here the most important ingredient is water.

The longer a flower drinks, the longer it lives. At La Grenouille, I change the water of each bouquet every morning. If I don't rearrange a large bouquet entirely, then I siphon the old water out completely and pour fresh water in. (If you do not know what siphoning is or how to do it, just ask a teenager what he does when his car runs out of gas.) Not only do crystal-clear vases sparkle with clean water but the flowers will live longer.

"... MA PAUVRE GISÈLE."

There are many products sold to maintain flowers longer. Some come in powder form, others in liquid. I find these helpful up to a point. But more important than anything else is the cleanliness of the water. Of course, the vase should be clean too.

Also be aware of the level of water; water evaporates and as the flowers drink, the water level lowers, sometimes beneath the tip of a flower's stem. When that happens, the flower no longer drinks; it is open to air and it dies. Why put all the effort into arranging a beautiful bouquet of flowers if you neglect to fill the vase sufficiently with water?

Another reason most flowers in a bouquet don't last is that they have not been properly conditioned. I have learned the hard way that if you don't spend time conditioning flowers before arranging them, you will waste a lot of flowers, time, and money.

When my father was in the hospital and I was about to start helping my mother with the restaurant, he spoke to me about quite a few things that were important to him, not least of which was the bouquets of the restaurant. He told me to cut the stems of carnations at an angle, remove the lower leaflets, and submerge the stems *up* to their heads in cool water. Once they drank the cool water it would be easy to make the blossoms open by bringing their container to a warmer place.

Papa told me to cut the stems of roses on a slant so they could drink more water. The lower leaves and thorns should be removed from the stem and the roses put immediately in a container with a little boiling water.

1. WITH A SHARP KNIFE CUT BOTTOM OF STEM ON A SLANT. REMOVE BY SCRAPING WITH THE SHARP KNIFE THE LEAVES AND THORNS THAT WOULD BE SUBMERGED IN WATER.

1.

He told me to smash and fray the woody stems of lilac and dogwood, and to cut off the white part of the lower stem of a tulip and take off the lower leaves. After removing most of the sand or dirt, the tulips should be placed in cold water.

Father told me a great deal about the flowers he loved so much. At first, I couldn't understand it all. It was so new to me. Put roses in a little bit of boiling water? I couldn't believe it until I tried it. He was right—as usual.

Since then, I have learned how to condition a few more flowers. I have made a lot of mistakes but I have learned from them. This is what I have learned so far:

Most flowers should be cut on a slant, so they can drink more (the more exposure to water, the better for almost every flower). The leaves and side shoots should be removed from the lower part of the stem, which will be submerged in water. This allows

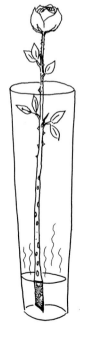

2. PLACE ROSE IN A TALL CONTAINER WITH A LITTLE BIT OF VERY HOT WATER. THE HOT WATER RISES TO THE FLOWER. REPEAT THIS STEP IF NECESSARY.

3. FILL THE CONTAINER WITH ROOM TEMPERATURE WATER UP TO THE FIRST THORNS OR LEAVES. FOR ONE GALLON OF WATER, USE ONE SMALL POUCH OF "CHRYSAL" POWDER OR 2 TABLESPOONS OF ALUM OR SALT. THE ROSE WILL NOW CONTINUE DRINKING THROUGH THE SUBMERGED OPENINGS.

2.

3.

SMASHING LILAC WITH A HAMMER.

the flower to drink more water through the openings under water, and it also keeps the water cleaner for a longer period of time. When removing the side shoots from the stem, keep these shoots in a small container full of water. They will eventually open up to be flowers in a smaller bouquet. It's important to use clean, sharp instruments when cutting the stems of flowers. If the blade is blunt, it will tear the stem rather than cutting it, which is bad for all flowers.

Branches such as apple blossom, dogwood, cherry, magnolia, peach, forsythia, mountain ash, and mountain laurel should be smashed with a hammer and frayed, or cut with pruners, cross-cutting the diameter.

The technique for conditioning most branches is to remove all of the dead shoots from the main branch. Clean the branch at the bottom by scraping off the bark. If a branch is forked, cut off those stems that you feel might draw water away from the main branch. Smash the bottom end of the branch with a hammer, or crosscut the branch with pruners.

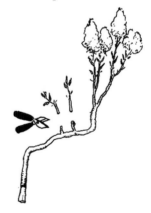

CUTTING A FORKED STEM.

Place the stem in a large container filled with water and add a flower nutrient such as Chrysal. Water temperature depends on the stage of the buds. If the buds are tight and you wish to force them open, use hot water and a smaller amount of it. You can repeat this step at several intervals, and you will notice a development. If the buds are about to open ("on the break"), the water should be at room temperature. If the buds are completely open, use a larger amount of cold water.

It's best to add 2 tablespoons of ammonia for each gallon of conditioning water, for apple blossom branches, to keep the water clean.

I have found that flowering camellia branches last two to three weeks. Flowering cherry blossoms last roughly two weeks. Dogwood can last from ten days to two weeks.

Magnolia, when the blossoms are tight, lasts one week. When the blossoms begin to open, count on three or four days at the most (and only if the room is kept cool and the water clean).

Mock orange blossom is temperamental. It can last five days, but if the room is a bit warm, it will shed immediately. Mountain laurel is very hardy and will last two or three weeks.

Flowering rhododendron lasts ten days to two weeks. The leaves seem to last forever!

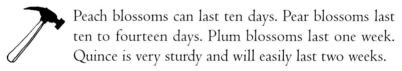

Peach blossoms can last ten days. Pear blossoms last ten to fourteen days. Plum blossoms last one week. Quince is very sturdy and will easily last two weeks.

Once the branch or flower is cleaned and conditioned, it needs to drink. I try to leave them overnight in the conditioning water in a cool place—the ideal temperature is 48°F.—and use them the following day in an arrangement with fresh water. Room temperature is important. Even after conditioning it is better to leave a bouquet of flowers in a cool place. Be sure to keep the bouquet away from heat sources such as a radiator or too much direct sunlight.

Whenever I cut a stem, I always cut above the node. If the stem is forked into several stems, I often cut them apart so they can each drink more water.

Flowers have a language of their own and each person has a different approach with flowers. The more one deals with flowers, the more personal it becomes. My father had unequaled success with tulips. His tulips lasted easily ten days. That must have taken a lot of talking!

Some of the treatments I have tried gave excellent results. Others didn't seem to make a significant difference. But then, the difference often lies in the person handling the flower rather than in the ingredients used or the flower itself. The flower usually tells you how it is through appearance and touch. It is CUTTING ABOVE THE NODE. impossible just with words to describe accurately when any flower is in the right condition to be used in an arrangement. If you are not sure about the look of a flower, touching it can help you sense its readiness.

When a flower is full of water, its stem, leaves, and blossom are firm. That's when the flower is ready to be used in a bouquet. Before inserting the flower in the arrangement, I give it one more fresh cut and immediately put it in the bouquet.

In addition to giving cut flowers as much water as they need to drink, it helps to nourish them too. I have revised a list of nourishing ingredients that was given to me by Judith Wyker, a dear friend of the family who was always there to help us. She knew more about flowers than anyone I have known. She helped my father in the beginning, and later, when I first worked at La Grenouille, she introduced me to the flower market and taught me a great deal about flowers. With time, I hope to see this list of ingredients grow.

Your personal judgment, feeling, and observation are important while using this list as a reference for conditioning flowers. Although the directions may be useful, they are not the whole secret to keeping cut flowers alive longer.

Just as what you put in the water is relevant, it is also crucial that the water should be clean and that whatever container you use for conditioning flowers should be neutral, such as glass or plastic, *never* metal.

The key to conditioning a cut flower is to revitalize it, to make it drink and return it to its original state before it was cut. The cut flower will require water, in appropriate amounts and temperatures. (Unless otherwise noted, the water should be at room temperature.) It will often need ingredients mixed in the water as well. When the flower drinks, it returns to life. If the flower doesn't drink, it stops developing and dies.

By appearance and touch you will know that the flower is alive and ready to be used in a bouquet. Most flowers should be cut on a slant to allow more surface area to be exposed to water. Straight cuts are for tubular stems or stems that look like straws, such as those of narcissus, daffodils, and anemones. Immediately after cutting the stem of a flower, place it in water; it is essential that air not enter the openings of the stem.

The conditioning mixtures are offered in a ratio; use the amount of water appropriate for the amount of flowers. And, for instance, the proportion of vinegar to water for a thick-stemmed lily should not be the same as for a thin-stemmed one.

ACHILLEA (YARROW)

2 tablespoons salt to 2 quarts water.

ACONITEM (MONKSHOOD)

$1\frac{1}{2}$ cups vinegar to 2 quarts water.

ALYSSUM

1 tablespoon sugar to 2 quarts water.

AMARYLLIS

2 teaspoons ammonia to 1 quart water. Cut stem straight across.

ANEMONE

Cut stem straight across. $\frac{1}{2}$ cup vinegar to 1 gallon water (less vinegar if the stem is weak). *Never spray.* If anemone in an arrangement droops, pull out, give fresh cut, and place in container filled with water and ice just up to base of the flower. Anemone will become firm and fresh again.

AQUILEGIA (COLUMBINE)

5 drops of oil of peppermint to 1 pint water.

ASCLEPIAS (BUTTERFLY WEED)

2 teaspoons sugar to 1 quart ice-cold water.

ASTER (ALL MEMBERS OF FAMILY)

2 tablespoons sugar plus 1 tablespoon salt to 1 quart water.

BEGONIA

2 tablespoons salt to 2 quarts water.

BIRD-OF-PARADISE
2 cups vinegar to 1 quart water.

BOCCONIA (PLUME POPPY)
Burn ends of stem. $\frac{1}{2}$ cup salt to 1 gallon water.

CAMELLIA
Keep moist; wrap in wet tissue overnight. These flowers never drink after being cut from the plant.

CAMPANULA (CANTERBURY BELL)
1 tablespoon baking soda to 1 quart water.

CARNATION
Cool water, just up to base of flower heads. To accelerate opening of blossoms, place container in a warm area for a short period of time.

CHRYSANTHEMUM
10 drops oil of cloves to two quarts water.

CLEMATIS
3 tablespoons alcohol and a pinch of baking soda to 1 quart water.

COREOPSIS
1 tablespoon salt to 1 quart water.

COSMOS
1 teaspoon sugar to 1 quart water.

DAFFODIL
Small quantities of water, for conditioning and otherwise.

DAHLIA
Burn ends of stems. 5 tablespoons alcohol to 3 quarts ice water.

DAISIES (ALL TYPES)

3 drops oil of peppermint to I
quart water.

REMOVE LEAVES AND SIDE SHOOTS
AT BOTTOM OF THE STEM: DON'T
CUT TOO CLOSE TO THE STEM.

DELPHINIUM

I tablespoon alcohol to I pint
water. With large hybrid del-
phiniums, carefully remove
lower side shoots from stem
with sharp knife, cutting not
too close to the stem. Turn delphinium upside down, cut stem
straight across, and fill hollow
stem with water mixed with
alcohol, as above. Plug opening
with cotton, turn flower right
side up, and immediately place
in a container full of water with
same proportion of alcohol.
Cotton plug allows water to
seep into stem so delphinium
can drink. Leave plug in when
using stems in a bouquet.

COTTON

WATER

PUT DELPHINIUM
UPSIDE DOWN.

FILL THE HOLLOW STEM
WITH WATER AND PLUG
THE OPENING WITH COTTON.

PLACE THE DELPHINIUM
RIGHT SIDE UP, IMMEDIATELY
IN CONTAINER OF WATER +
ALCOHOL.

DIGITALIS
I tablespoon alcohol to I pint water.

EUPHORBIA
Burn ends of stems. A handful of salt to 2 quarts cold water.

EVERGREENS (ALL TYPES)
I tablespoon glycerine to I quart water.

FERNS
Submerge under water completely for 12 hours. When ready to use, shake well.

FORGET-ME-NOT
Plunge stems into hot water, then cold water containing 3 drops alcohol to I pint water.

FUNKIA (DAY LILY)
$\frac{1}{2}$ cup vinegar to 2 cups cold water.

GAILLARDIA
2 tablespoons salt to I pint water.

GARDENIA
See camellia.

GLADIOLUS
5 tablespoons vinegar to I quart water.

GRAPE HYACINTH
Plunge stems into hot water, then cold water containing 3 drops alcohol to I pint water.

GYPSOPHILIA (BABY'S BREATH)
I teaspoon alcohol to I pint water.

HOLLYHOCK
Burn ends of stems. A handful of salt to 2 quarts water.

HYACINTH
Squeeze substance from end of stems, preferably as soon as blossom is picked. Plunge stem immediately into very cold water. Add 5 drops oil of peppermint.

IRIS
3 drops oil of peppermint to 1 quart water.

LARKSPUR
1 tablespoon alcohol to 1 pint water.

LILAC
Crush bottom of stem. Use Chrysal powder mixed with cold water. Never pull off green leaf at top, near flowering head; it is the water conductor to the blossom.

LILIES
½ cup vinegar to 1 gallon water. Less vinegar if stem is thin or weak. Remove pollen from flower by pulling gently.

MARIGOLD
2 tablespoons sugar plus 1 tablespoon salt to 1 quart water.

MILKWEED
Burn end of stem. A handful of salt to 2 quarts water.

MIMOSA
Remove lower leaves. Place in container with shallow hot water and 2 tablespoons sugar and cover with plastic bag. Steam will help mimosa develop. Step can be repeated several times.

NARCISSUS (ALL MEMBERS OF FAMILY)
Small quantity of water for conditioning and otherwise.

PEONY
Rush water to blossoms by putting in a little bit of hot water, then in 1 pint water with 3 tablespoons sugar. Keep in a cool place at all times; peonies wilt quickly in heat.

PETUNIA
1 teaspoon sugar to 1 pint water.

PLATYCODON (BALLOON-FLOWER)
$\frac{1}{2}$ cup vinegar to 1 gallon water.

POINSETTIA
Burn ends of stems. A handful of salt to 2 quarts cold water.

POPPY
Burn ends of stems. A handful of salt to 2 quarts water.

ROSE
Remove lower leaves and thorns on part of stem that will be submerged in water. Rush water to flower by putting in a container with a little boiling water. When flower is firm and leaves and petals have new life, add 1 gallon room-temperature water with 2 tablespoons powdered alum Chrysal powder, or salt.

SALVIA (SAGE)
1 tablespoon alcohol to 1 pint water.

SNAPDRAGON
2 tablespoons salt to 2 quarts water. Pinch off top budlet with your fingers.

STATICE
3 tablespoons sugar to 1 quart water.

TULIP
Cut off white part of lower stem, remove lower leaves, scrape off sand or dirt. Place tulips in shallow warm water with $\frac{1}{2}$ tablespoon sugar to 1 quart water. Flowers will open and bend graciously.

Judith would place tulips in cold water up to the flower heads. Roll in wet newspapers if you wish to keep stems straight.

VIOLA AND VIOLETS
Submerge entire flower in water for 1 hour, then place in container filled with ice water and allow to warm to room temperature.

WATER LILY (NYMPHAEA) AND LOTUS
12 drops alcohol to 1 pint water. Submerge completely in the water for a few hours.

Flowers are living creatures, needing care. The most important ingredient of all, before any of these ingredients listed above, is water. But even more important than that is the *person* handling the flower. All the knowledge in the world about flowers won't help if you handle flowers like old rags.

I have seen my daughter Flavia, my son Charlie, and my wife Francesca make flower arrangements for our house, with no knowledge whatsoever of the things mentioned in this chapter. They do it with loving care, and that makes all the difference. When my father asked if the flowers were spoken to, it may have seemed odd, but he wasn't kidding.

It makes a big difference how you treat flowers. The difference was certainly visible in my father's bouquets.

A LABOR
OF
LOVE

My father used plants and herbs judiciously for cooking and believed that their proper use is essential for good health. In some instances, they are the natural cures of some illnesses. My father knew well the plants that he loved so much.

When Papa spoke enthusiastically of flowers and plants, there were people, as there are still today, who thought that all of this talk about flowers, plants, and herbs was strange. Unfortunately, most florists would go out of business were it not for weddings and funerals.

When my father first put flowers so profusely throughout his restaurant, it was at a time when restaurants almost invariably chose to place not more than a blossom or two in a bud vase on each table. Larger bouquets were hardly seen; they were deemed inappropriate for a dining establishment. The aroma and exuberance of large bouquets were considered a distraction rather than an enhancement to dining.

"Il faut cultiver son jardin."

"One must cultivate one's garden."

—Voltaire

My father was a pioneer. Through the restaurant he showed what flowers could do. And, thank goodness, many people have been directly or indirectly inspired by his work. Yet occasionally there are customers who, after dining in our restaurant, still cannot believe that the flowers are real.

My father's philosophy on cooking could be summed up in one word: freshness. You use fresh ingredients—herbs, vegetables, fruits, fish, meat—and you create a spontaneously fresh cuisine, with no camouflage. What else could embody this ideal better than to have fresh-cut flowers every day in the restaurant?

"OF COURSE, THE FLOWERS AREN'T REAL."

I cannot imagine how we would feel if one day there were no flowers. It is never too late to learn the pleasures of planting and watering a tree, the rewards and virtues of herbs and plants in cooking and healing, or the pleasure of making a bouquet of flowers. These are small accomplishments, perhaps, but they are rewarding, not just for ourselves but for those generations that follow and who may learn from us.

When the kings of France planted oak trees, they did not do it for themselves, since oak do not reach adult size for fifty years. Instead, they planted them for their children, their successors, and the generations that would follow. Planting an oak tree is an unselfish act.

You need not be a king to appreciate and take part in this ritual which makes your life and the life of those around you, and especially those after you, more beautiful. My mother and father planted their own oak tree when they first opened the doors of La Grenouille.

Flowers are not only for the gardener, the artist, or the eccentric—they are for those fortunate enough to live fully every moment of their life. I hear people complain that flowers don't last forever. What we all like to forget is that *nothing* lasts forever. All things come to an end. That is what makes flowers real. When the first flowers pierce the earth in the spring, they, too, remind us that even winter comes to an end.

I would rather stroll through a tree-lined lane than walk on an asphalt street. A yard of trees and flowering plants is more inviting to me than a fenced enclosure of dirt. I would rather live in a house with flowers than in one without them.

If you believe that "you are what you eat," you might also agree that you are what you see. A diet of only junk food will make you sick to the stomach, and if only ugliness surrounds you, it could make you sick at heart. For those of us living in cities of concrete and steel where there is little room for trees and the sky is often seen in geometric patches, aesthetics are confined, if not limited. Since urban living does not offer too many of us an opportunity for a real garden of our own, our garden can be created with flowers in the house. Nor does it have to cost an arm and a leg to have a few fresh blooms. The ensuing happiness is worth much more than one can imagine.

And when the restaurant opens its doors so early in the morning, throughout the seasons, with so many flowers, it is only the introduction to a daily ritual; a labor of love, never a mechanical routine. It is the fresh creation of what is on the plate and around it. It is a daily feast, the celebration of life.

ACKNOWLEDGMENTS

I thank Peter Brown and Alexandra Stoddard Brown, for without their encouragement and their belief in me, this book would have remained a project.

My deepest gratitude to Wendy Goodman for helping me write this book and to Oberto Gili for his photographs and his patience. To all my friends, and to Carl Brandt, Katie Workman, Lauren Shakely, Howard Klein, Maggie Hinders, and all the many others who have made this book possible.

To Maman, Francesca, Flavia, Charlie, and Philippe with love.